IMAGES
of America

CHARDON AND
CHARDON TOWNSHIP

Peter Chardon Brooks, a wealthy Boston landowner, sold the property for the village square of the town that would bear his middle name. This bust was sculpted in 1849, the year of Brooks's death. Records indicate that Brooks never visited the town that bears his name. The bust—a gift from the Brooks family during the Chardon sesquicentennial—is displayed in the Chardon municipal building.

ON THE COVER: A group of young berry-pickers is shown on the Sage farm about 1900. In the early years, agriculture was the primary occupation in Chardon Township, with support provided by a number of Chardon Village businesses. The Sage farm is still in operation today. (From the collection of the Sage family.)

IMAGES
of America

CHARDON AND
CHARDON TOWNSHIP

Debbie Chuha, Bill Jackson, and Joan Windnagel for the
Chardon Bicentennial Celebration Steering Committee

ARCADIA
PUBLISHING

Published by Arcadia Publishing
Charleston, South Carolina

Library of Congress Control Number: 2011932798

For all general information, please contact Arcadia Publishing:
Telephone 843-853-2070
Fax 843-853-0044
E-mail sales@arcadiapublishing.com
For customer service and orders:
Toll-Free 1-888-313-2665

Visit us on the Internet at www.arcadiapublishing.com

CONTENTS

ACKNOWLEDGMENTS

One of the most rewarding experiences for the authors in preparing this pictorial history has been the cooperation they have received from members of the Chardon, Geauga County, and Lake County communities in finding photographs, identifying images, and offering suggestions for improving the product. We were fortunate to have a number of public sources and private collections from which to select many of the photographs in this book. However, the willingness of individuals and families to search through their albums and attics for fascinating pictures has made this effort special.

The public sources have been invaluable in allowing access to the photographic images they have painstakingly collected over many years. We thank the Geauga County Archives, the Geauga County Historical Society, the Lake County Historical Society, the Geauga County Public Library, the Geauga County Engineer's Office, the Chardon Chamber of Commerce, the City of Chardon, and the Township of Chardon for their willingness to open their archives to the authors.

Joseph Spear, who began preserving the photographic history of our town and township decades ago, is to be commended for the success of his efforts and for his unrestricted permission to use his collection. Many other contributors have graciously responded to appeals for help in finding the most representative local photographs. In alphabetical order, we thank the Allyn family, Bill and Linda Arotin, Jan Began, the Bender family, Patricia Fisher Benedict, Robert Bowyer, Anna Lee Bryan, Marc and Nan Burr, the Carmigiano family, Robert Clark, the Cleveland & Eastern Interurban Historical Society and Museum, Doris Cook, the Crombie family, Beth and Jim Croup, the DeFilippo family, Priscilla Eldredge, Jan Farinacci, the Finley family, Chris Freno, Cathy Gillette, Jeanette "Teeter" Grosvenor, Wendy Guion, Beth Halasz, David Jevnikar, Betty and Joseph Koelliker, Barbara and Milton Luther, Kaye and Harve Lyon, the Mansfield family, Patricia Martin, Cheryl McClellan, Betty Meyer, Norma Moses, Thomas Offutt, the Pentek family, Ellen Peska, Shirley Pokorny, the Post family, John Reithoffer, Nancy Rhodes, the Richards family, the Rickard family, the Rusnak family, the Sage family, Robert Schnittger, Karen Simpson, Rob and Mary Ann Smith, Nancy Speck, Dorothy Stange, Struna Galleries, Betty Talcott, Mary Alice Taylor, Bonnie Thayer, Jerry Tvergyak, Loretta and Arbin Vaughn, Dottie Wedge, Stephen Wick, and Fred Wilder. Our apologies are extended to anyone who we may have unintentionally omitted from this list of contributors.

INTRODUCTION

Established in 1812, the Township of Chardon was the first governmental unit to be formed from the land now encompassing the City of Chardon and Chardon Township. During this same period, the clearing and settlement of Chardon Hill was taking place, although the Village of Chardon was not incorporated until 1851.

Peter Chardon Brooks, a wealthy merchant from Boston, and his partner Nathaniel Gorham purchased 6,684 acres of land, constituting the whole of Tract 3 in Chardon Township, from the trustees of the Connecticut Land Company in September 1798. Less than a year later, Brooks bought out Gorham's interest in the land. In September 1809, Brooks provided power of attorney to Simon Perkins to sell his Ohio land. In September 1811, Brooks, acting through Perkins, sold part of Tract 3 for $400 to Samuel Phelps, director of the Chardon town plat. The land was purchased for the establishment of a seat of local government. In agreeing to this transaction, it is said that Brooks requested that the place be named Chardon in memory of Peter Chardon, a close friend of Brooks's father. The word "chardon" is French for thistle.

In 2012, the City of Chardon and Chardon Township will celebrate their collective 200th anniversary. A committee of citizens was formed in late 2010 to plan a bicentennial celebration. This committee quickly identified a pictorial history book as a project that it wished to undertake as part of this effort. Although two major histories of Geauga County have been written and a pictorial history of the county was compiled a couple of decades ago, Chardon was only a piece of these works and had not been the subject of a history book solely dedicated to the township and city. The committee sought volunteers from the community and identified three interested parties as the authors.

The authors have sought to collect as many old photographs of the area as possible. From the beginning, we have targeted photos that are at least 50 years old, emphasizing our desire to obtain as much early photographic documentation as possible. Thankfully, many folks who came before us recorded local history in photographs and subsequently donated these images to local preservation groups. We deem ourselves truly fortunate to have access to such a large array of informative and quality historical photographs. To that end, you will find very few recent pictures within the book, even though more recent images might be familiar and even intimate to our readers.

Chardon has a rich and varied history that begins with its agricultural roots. Somewhat isolated by topography and weather, Chardon first developed as a farming community. The area's early businesses and industries were established to support the majority of its population, who were engaged in farming, timbering, and other livelihoods based on the land. With few exceptions, Chardon Township has never been commercially developed. Beginning with family farms, it has gradually been repopulated with the residences of people who work in neighboring towns and the suburbs of Cleveland. As the county seat of Geauga County, the City of Chardon became a hub of government activity, including the supporting cast of attorneys, title and insurance companies, and real estate agencies. It also developed as the retail and commercial center of northern Geauga

County, as well as the home of a number of small industrial companies. While many residents of the city work for local businesses, many others commute to jobs in other communities. It is hoped that the selected photographs will give a sense of Chardon's small-town past and its change to a less agriculturally dependent community. At the same time, we hope to portray a community that has enjoyed steady growth mixed with tragedy and triumph. Finally, we seek to show a town that is proud of its own heritage and pleased with its surroundings.

The authors have identified three local topics of note that have become chapters in this book—the maple syrup industry, the winter weather for which Chardon is well known, and the Chardon Centennial Celebration. The book also highlights the variety of businesses that have been part of the life of this community over the years and the activities that have been part of the fabric of this town and township, including its decidedly patriotic character.

Having initiated this effort at the beginning of the anniversary celebration, it is hoped that this book will generate a strong interest in Chardon's past and stimulate still others to rummage through family albums, steamer trunks, and hiding places to find more dramatic images. We encourage everyone to come forward and share his or her findings. It is our hope that Chardon's bicentennial year will yield a bountiful crop of old documents and photographs to add to the public treasure trove of local history. The authors intend to serve as collectors of this information now and through the next year.

One

LOCAL AND COUNTY GOVERNMENT

The layers of government administering the lands of Chardon and Chardon Township were created in a top-down chronological sequence. The state of Ohio came into being in 1803. In 1805, Geauga County was carved out of Jefferson County, Ohio. In 1812, the Township of Chardon was formally established and became one of about 24 townships within the county. At that time, Geauga County also included the land that later became Lake County, Ohio. For the next 39 years, Chardon Township was the sole governmental unit over this land, even as the small but growing settlement of Chardon became the seat of county government. In 1851, the Village of Chardon was incorporated. Following the 2000 census, Chardon Village became a city, since the population exceeded 5,000 people for the first time.

As the seat of Geauga County, Chardon serves as the center of many of the offices and functions of county government. Currently, many of the departments of county government are located in a complex of buildings on Center Street, while the county courts and the offices of most elected county officials are located on and next to Chardon Square.

The first Geauga County Courthouse was originally built in 1812 on Chardon Square. The building was only used for a couple of years. The replica shown here was built for the Geauga County centennial in 1905 and was placed on the southwest corner of Chardon Square's north park during the celebration. (From the collection of Joe Spear.)

The third Geauga County Courthouse was located on the west side of Main Street, just north of the mouth of Court Street. The building was erected about 1824, completed over several years, and survived until the devastating fire of 1868 that destroyed much of Main Street. Before it burned, the building housed most county offices, including the jail. (From the collection of Joe Spear.)

This photograph shows Chardon's first police chief John Bohl in the late 1940s greeting school children at Park Elementary School. The Village of Chardon established a full-time police department in June 1947 with John Bohl as chief and Joseph Dorko and Louis Robusky as patrolmen. Before then the village was served by part-time personnel. (From the collection of Chardon Chamber of Commerce.)

This is a view of the 1869 courthouse soon after its completion. The image shows an open, post–Civil War Chardon Square. The courthouse was inspected and accepted by the Geauga County commissioners on August 20, 1870. The Wilbur house, the middle white frame building on the right, survived until the early 2000s, when it was demolished after an unsuccessful campaign to save it. (From the collection of Joe Spear.)

This view of the courthouse shows three forms of transportation used during the second decade of the 20th century. The electric interurban car made a loop on a track around the southern half of Chardon Square, the early panel truck delivered goods to one of the local merchants, and the horse and wagon carried goods purchased by a local farmer. (From the collection of Fred Wilder.)

A group of mail carriers, with the post office behind them, line up with their Model T cars before heading out on their rural routes. At the time, the post office was located in the Bickle building on the north end of Main Street, near the second Chardon Methodist Church. The offices of two competing local newspapers, the *Geauga Republican* and the *Geauga Record*, were housed in the same building. (From the collection of Karen Simpson.)

Chardon's first freestanding post office was this early 1940s Art Deco structure built by the Public Works Administration on South Street. The building served as the post office until 1984, when it was replaced by the current structure on the northeast corner of Center and Washington Streets. The building shown here has subsequently been used by the public library, the Red Cross, and an accounting firm. (From the collection of Bill Jackson.)

The original Chardon Town Hall, built about 1860, stood on the site of the present courthouse. The town hall was moved to the East Park Street site in 1869 when the present (fourth) courthouse was being built. In 1908, Lloyd McNaughton purchased the retired town hall structure, dismantled it, and moved it to its present location at a private residence on Claridon Road. (From the collection of Joe Spear.)

This is a view of the old city hall, taken soon after its construction. Built in 1908, this building served as the administrative offices of the village for about 80 years. The D.F. Avery grocery store is visible at right. Today, this building serves as the home of the Chardon Fire Department. (From the collection of Bill Jackson.)

This is a photograph of the Geauga County jail when it was located on Main Street, to the west of the courthouse. This building not only housed the jail, it also served as the residence and office of the Geauga County sheriff. (From the collection of Joe Spear.)

The members of the first full-time Chardon Village Police Department are pictured here around 1950. From left to right, they are John Bohl, chief of police; Louis Robusky; Walter Bookman; and Michael Fisher. (From the collection of Joe Spear.)

Members of the Chardon Village Volunteer Fire Department—and the department's early fire engine—are seen here in front of the village hall and fire station at the south end of Chardon Square. (From the collection of Joe Spear.)

This c. 1900 image shows county recorder F.E. Ford and his assistant, Lizzie Reynolds, inside the recorder's office in the Geauga County Courthouse. Note the regulator clock on the wall and the manual typewriter and book press behind the public officials—no telephones or computers in sight and few papers being processed. (From the collection of Joe Spear.)

The new Chardon Township building was under construction in 1993. Prior to that time, Chardon Township had no dedicated home. At various times, it held meetings in the Chardon Village Hall, the courthouse annex, a local bank, and the meetinghouse on Chardon Square. (From the collection of Chardon Township.)

Two

MAIN STREET

Throughout most of Chardon's 200-year history, Main Street has hosted most of its retail and commercial activity. This street has been the home of numerous grocers, hardware dealers, department stores, banks, barbers, and lawyers. It was the chosen location of hotels, meeting halls, fraternal groups, and governmental offices. Although in recent years it has become less of a retail and commercial hub, efforts have been made to encourage businesses that attract local residents and visitors to Chardon Square. Today, restaurants, antique shops, and locally owned specialty retailers and service businesses populate the storefronts.

This early photograph shows business row on Main Street. The pillared building at right, with the rounded cupola, is the 1824 courthouse. The first section of the courthouse was constructed about 1824 and the second section in 1828 or 1829. The cupola was added in 1845. On the right and nearly indistinguishable at the street's north end is the Brick Hotel, also known as the "old stone tavern," destroyed by fire on January 28, 1871, shortly after this photograph was taken. (From the collection of Joe Spear.)

This composite image shows Main Street before the Great Fire of July 1868. The 1824–1829 courthouse at right was the third of four county courthouses. The first courthouse, an 1812 log cabin, was located on the southeast corner of Chardon Square. The second courthouse, built in 1813, was a two-story log-and-frame structure on Main Street, near Water Street. (From the collection of Joe Spear.)

This photograph depicts the aftermath of the disastrous fire of July 25, 1868. This calamity destroyed virtually all retail and commercial buildings on Chardon's Main Street, as well as the courthouse. Only the wood-framed Chardon Methodist Church, toward the north end of the street, on the right, escaped the flames. The village's citizens quickly resolved to rebuild and began to formulate plans to replace these ruins. (From the collection of Joe Spear.)

This structure was known as the Beehives. It was built at the south end of Chardon Square immediately after the fire of 1868 to temporarily house the essential businesses of Chardon while new Main Street buildings were under construction. (From the collection of Betty Koelliker.)

Following the fire of July 25, 1868, there was an immediate determination to rebuild Main Street. This photograph shows the construction of the Randall Block, on the south end of Main Street, within a year of the fire. The block was named for L.J. Randall, owner of several enterprises that soon occupied these storefronts. A third story, added in 1879, became the Independent Order of Odd Fellows (IOOF) Hall. (From the collection of Joe Spear.)

Here is another early photograph of the reconstructed Main Street buildings following the devastating fire of 1868. Note the planked sidewalks crossing the street. Main Street was not paved until about 1903, so mud was a problem after heavy rains and winter thaws. When this photograph was taken, there was not yet a third floor on the Randall Block. (From the collection of Dottie Wedge.)

This view of Main Street was taken from just south of Water Street. Note the drainage ditches that lined the street, which attempted to draw water from the unpaved and frequently muddy roadway. This photograph predates 1900, as there is no track of the Cleveland & Eastern electric railroad looping around the southern half of Chardon Square. (From the collection of Joe Spear.)

The Memorial Block housed the Parks and Barker Hardware Store, the post office, and Chardon's newspapers, the *Geauga Republican* and the *Geauga Record*. The newspapers espoused different political views, although their copy was run on the same press. The Grand Army of the Republic (GAR) Memorial Hall on the third floor honored the veterans of the Civil War and held many fraternal and patriotic meetings. (From the collection of Joe Spear.)

This is the first of eight wonderful compass point views taken around 1900 from the clock tower of the Geauga County Courthouse. This view looks due north along North Street. Note the lack of development away from Chardon Square, the amount of open space, and the lack of trees. Much of the forest had been timbered, and these trees represent second growth plantings. (From the collection of Joe Spear.)

Here is the second compass view from the courthouse, looking northeast. There was little building on Maple Avenue at this time, as evidenced by the open fields and lack of houses. (From the collection of Joe Spear.)

The third compass view from the courthouse looks east. The Chardon Town Hall is on the left and the first consolidated school building, known as Union School, is on the right. The school included all grades from one through 12 and was the home of the first local high school. (From the collection of Joe Spear.)

The fourth compass view from the courthouse looks southeast. A number of stately houses on East Park and South Hambden Streets are visible in this photograph. The Chardon Baptist Church is in the foreground at left. It was the first church organized in Chardon. The tracks of the Cleveland & Eastern electric railroad are visible in the right foreground. (From the collection of Joe Spear.)

The fifth compass view from the courthouse looks south. This photograph overlooks the southern half of Chardon Square. The loop of the electric interurban railroad track is on the perimeter of the park, with a blurred interurban car in motion at right. The Chardon House hotel is shown in the upper right, and the open hills south of the village are in the background. (From the collection of Joe Spear.)

The sixth compass view from the courthouse looks southwest, showing the Opera House and the entrance to Court Street as it opens onto Main Street. Many houses can be seen on the western slope of the village, indicating that much early growth was on the west side of town. (From the collection of Joe Spear.)

The seventh compass view from the courthouse looks west, with the GAR Memorial Hall in the foreground, flanked by a windmill. The windmill pumped water that was used for a public drinking fountain and a watering trough for horses. (From the collection of Joe Spear.)

The eighth and last compass view from the courthouse looks northwest. The second Methodist Church is visible on the corner of Center and Main Streets. Again, there are open fields in the distance, with none of the industries that later occupied this land. (From the collection of Joe Spear.)

Taken on a quiet day on Main Street, this image shows the offices of Chardon Savings Bank, a longtime local financial institution. It is the first storefront to the left of the long white awning. The bank independently survived until the 1980s, when it was purchased by Bank One. On the right, the Cleveland & Eastern electric railroad track circles the southern half of Chardon Square. In the right background, the Park Hotel can be seen at the north end of Main Street. Chardon Savings Bank later relocated to the site of the Park Hotel. (From the collection of Joe Spear.)

This c. 1910 photograph offers a view of Main Street on a busy shopping day. The street is lined with sleighs and bobsleds, and an electric railway car is idling on the loop around the southern half of Chardon Square. (From the collection of Joe Spear.)

This picture offers a view of Main Street that is very similar to the previous image, but this photograph was taken about two decades later. The facades of the buildings have changed and most stores have been replaced by a new set of merchants. On this busy day, automobiles line both sides of the streets. (From the collection of Patricia Fisher Benedict.)

An aerial photograph of Chardon Square taken in the 1930s shows the development of the village at that time. Note the two-way traffic on Main Street, the original and second high school buildings in the middle of the picture on the right, and the water tower in the foreground. These features have all disappeared over time. (From the collection of Priscilla Eldredge.)

Main Street was active in the early 1950s. Rickard's Bakery, a fixture on Main Street, is on the far left. A delivery truck brought produce to a grocery store on the block. Through the 1960s, Main Street remained the primary retail center of Chardon Village and Township. Parking on both sides of the street indicates two-way traffic. (From the collection of Bill Jackson.)

This photograph from the 1960s shows Julie's store, the Ben Franklin Store, and other retail establishments frequented by the Chardon community. Although the names of many businesses changed over the years, up until the 1960s, Main Street remained the place to shop. (From the collection of the Struna Galleries.)

Three

STREETS AND RESIDENCES

Chardon and Chardon Township have a number of charming features, including the tree-lined roadways and streets and the rolling hills that lend variety and contrast to the landscape. Chardon Square sits on top of a hill, and the connecting streets that spoke away from it in all directions are sloped. From its earliest history, Chardon was blessed with an abundant cover of trees. As timbering took place and old growth died off, concerted efforts were made to replant trees so as to maintain the pleasant surroundings. For many years, the City of Chardon has been recognized for both its "green" environment and its programs that support the replenishing of tree stock.

Chardon Township also contains numerous picturesque scenes. Many of its acres are now preserved in a natural state through ownership by the Geauga County Park District and the Holden Arboretum, as well as holdings by significant private estates. The reclaimed railroad right-of-way, now a bicycling and walking path, provides an opportunity to enjoy nature. Recently, the township itself acquired land for an active-use township park.

The images in this chapter depict a number of the streets in the village during bygone days. Many of the homes in these views have been preserved, and there are nearly 500 homes in Chardon and Chardon Township that date back at least 100 years.

This 1910 photograph of Chardon Hill was taken from the west. At the bottom of the hill, railroad cars rest near the Chardon depot. The crest of the hill is dominated by the Geauga County Courthouse tower and the spire of the Congregational Church (now the Pilgrim Christian Church). (From the collection of Bill Jackson.)

This view, looking northward from just north of Claridon Road, shows South Street, with the courthouse tower visible in the distance. South Street was paved about 1908. This postcard was postmarked in 1911. The Cleveland & Eastern interurban railroad track and its overhead electric wire can be seen on the side of the street as it heads up the hill to Chardon Square. (From the collection of Bill Jackson.)

This photograph of North Street shows a number of houses on the west side of the street immediately south of Fifth Avenue. North and South Streets, along with the streets flowing east and west off Chardon Square, contain many of the over 350 century homes located in the city. (From the collection of Bill Jackson.)

This early view of Center Street features a horse and buggy climbing the hill to Chardon Square. Many wood-frame houses line the street behind a fairly uniform row of moderate-growth trees. The road, although unpaved at the time, was curbed. Center Street is now a section of Ohio Route 44 and carries a large volume of traffic into Chardon from the north. (From the collection of Bill Jackson.)

This is a view of Court Street near Chardon Square. The first houses on the left and right no longer exist, having been torn down to create retail, commercial, and governmental parking lots. Court Street did not extend to Chardon Square until after the 1868 fire, but it did connect the commercial district with the railroad depot at the bottom of the hill. (From the collection of the DeFilippo family.)

Water Street is seen here in a less busy era. A child is walking a bicycle up the hill to Chardon Square as two horse-drawn buggies negotiate the rise. At the bottom of the hill, cross bucks indicate the location of the railroad tracks. The hillside to the west is no longer such a pastoral setting, as it is now filled with retail and commercial establishments, as well as housing complexes. (From the collection of Bill Jackson.)

This photograph shows the homes of the Patchin family, on the left, and Doctors Clara Swan and Lucy Stone Hertzog, on the right. The doctors were female physicians who practiced in Chardon for a number of years. The women also grew ginseng, a valuable herbal root used for medicinal and dietary purposes. During the early 20th century, Chardon was a significant producer of ginseng. (From the collection of Joe Spear.)

This view, looking southeast from the outbound hill on Claridon Road (also known as Aquilla Road), shows the road and hillside graded in preparation for paving. After this construction project was completed, the section of Claridon Road from Chardon Village to south of Aquilla Village represented the first macadam or asphalt road in the area. (From the collection of Joe Spear.)

This is a photograph of the Cooley residence on Chardon-Mentor Road. This homestead, one of the oldest residences in the township, has been in the Cooley family for over 150 years. This c. 1908 photograph includes, from left to right, Carlos, Melbert (standing in rear), Rella (holding Harlan), and Thelma Cooley. (From the collection of Barbara and Milton Luther.)

This is a residence at Mountain Glen Farm. In the early 1900s, the McMillan family purchased a number of smaller farms to create Mountain Glen Farm, an operation that continues today. (From the collection of Thomas Offutt.)

Four

BUSINESS, INDUSTRY, AND TRANSPORTATION

Much of Chardon's history can be retold through revisiting its businesses and industries. Although many livelihoods in Chardon Township were based on agriculture, farm families exchanged crops and animal products for other needed goods. For most households, Chardon Village was the center of commercial activity, whether that meant barter, sale, or shipping.

Chardon has been blessed with many types of enterprises and an interesting mix of locally produced goods and services—some with long lives and some fleeting endeavors. The following images offer a glimpse of these businesses over the years.

This c. 1868 photograph of the original wood-framed Chardon House hotel shows a large audience listening to an unknown speaker. The original building burned in a fire in 1878. From its earliest days, this hotel was a major center of town activity. (From the collection of Joe Spear.)

This view of Water Street from the south end of Chardon Square looks west. The building on the left was still named the Chardon House. This brick structure had its grand opening on October 15, 1879, after an earlier wood-frame hotel was destroyed by fire. This hotel housed Chardon's visiting businessmen and travelers and hosted many dances and events. (From the collection of Bill Jackson.)

The Chardon House was purchased by new owners in 1912 and renamed the Highland Hotel. The Highland Hotel was demolished in 1938. This photograph shows a leafless tree, probably in springtime, and an advertisement for maple syrup. A sign in the background advertises Burr and Smith Furniture. (From the collection of Bill Jackson.)

This c. 1920 image shows the livery stable located off South Street, behind the Highland Hotel. This business served Chardon's "horse-powered" visitors for many years. (From the collection of Joe Spear.)

This view from South Street shows the back of the Highland Hotel in the 1930s. By this time, the local electric railroad had been dismantled and buses were used for public and private transportation. (From the collection of the Geauga County Archives.)

Following the removal of the Highland Hotel, L.M. Smith built the Geauga Theater in 1938 and opened it in February 1939. For many years, the theater was owned and operated by Carl Brinkman. This one-screen movie theater served Chardon until 1997, when it ceased being a movie house and became the home of the Geauga Lyric Theatre Guild, which stages several live productions each year. (From the collection of Bill Jackson.)

Before the freestanding movie theater was built in 1938, Chardon residents could see motion pictures at the Opera House. Here, the marquee advertises a pair of movies, *Down on the Farm* and *West of the Santa Fe*. (From the collection of Fred Wilder.)

This view of the Park Hotel, located on the northwest corner of Chardon Square, shows Crandall (left) and Hayden Hendershott in a cart. The Park Hotel competed with the Highland Hotel and later became an apartment building. (From the collection of Joe Spear.)

The Park Hotel had a number of owners and a succession of names before being converted to apartments. (From the collection of Joe Spear.)

The Chardon electric power plant was on Cemetery Street, also known as Park Avenue, near the railroad tracks. In the early 20th century, this plant provided the electricity needed to light the businesses and homes of the village. It was replaced by the services provided by the Cleveland Illuminating Company. (From the collection of the DeFilippo family.)

A coal train rests in Chardon in the early 1940s, with its steam engine belching out black clouds of coal smoke. The powerful Mallet locomotives pulled long trains and negotiated the relatively steep grade from Fairport Harbor to Chardon, which once served as a staging location for the trains. At least one early map shows the railroad yard being 12 tracks wide. (From the collection of Joe Spear.)

This photograph shows a coal train at the Chardon railroad yard. The engine is a Mallet, with two lead wheels, two sets of eight driver wheels, and four trail wheels; in railroading terms, a 2-8-8-4. The identifying number for the engine is believed to be 7309. The railroad connected the port of Fairport Harbor to the steel mills of the Mahoning Valley and the coal mines of West Virginia and southeastern Ohio. The railroad's heavy two-way flow of bulk materials long justified its existence. (From the collection of Joe Spear.)

The Chardon depot for the Baltimore and Ohio Railroad is seen here as it appeared in the 1950s. Primarily used for freight, the depot and local industrial spurs received raw materials intended for Chardon's industries and sent out the goods that these industries and the local farms produced. (From the collection of Bill Jackson.)

The engines of a B&O freight train cross Water Street and head to the southeast, one of the last B&O trains to run through Chardon before the line was abandoned by the railroad on November 1, 1981. Some of the old B&O railroad right-of-way is now the Maple Highlands bicycle and walking trail, owned and maintained by the Geauga County Park District. (From the collection of Joe Spear.)

This view shows the old Chardon Macaroni Company factory from the southwest. This manufacturer of macaroni noodles operated from 1902 until World War I. Many of its workers were foreign-born or first-generation Italian-Americans. The company closed because the war cut off an adequate supply of flour. The building later housed the Chardon Rubber Company. (From the collection of the DeFilippo family.)

The Chardon Rubber Company was undoubtedly the largest employer in Chardon's history. Founded in 1919, the company continued under several owners until its closure in May 2009. A large number of employees still recall their labor at this company. Chardon Custom Polymers has resumed producing a line of products similar to those made by Chardon Rubber Company. (From the collection of Bill Jackson.)

During World War II, the Snapout Forms Company exclusively contracted with the federal government to produce many types of forms required for the war effort. (From the collection of Bill Jackson.)

The Chardon Brick and Tile plant sat at the foot of Claridon Road. The railroad right-of-way can be seen in the background. While local brick was not the area's primary building material, it was used for many homes and businesses. Prior to 1900, much of Chardon's industry was located on the east side of town. After that time, it shifted to the west side. (From the collection of the Geauga County Archives.)

44

Here are the owners and workers of Parks and Barker Hardware Store. From left to right, they are Jack Toop, Charlie Stevenson, Orrin Parks, Charlie Young, and Charles Parks. Among other products, the company was well known for its tin evaporators, used in the production of maple syrup. (From the collection of the Geauga County Archives.)

The interior of Parks and Barker, located in the northern commercial block of Main Street, is seen here. Most items in the store appear to be made of metal—many of these products were likely made in the company's tin shop. Parks and Barker supplied gallon containers to the area's maple syrup producers and milk cans to farmers. (From the collection of Joe Spear.)

In this c. 1912 photograph, a large crowd gathers in front of Parks and Barker to view a demonstration of a "modern" washing machine. The pillared building in the background, built a few years earlier, served as the Geauga County sheriff's office, sheriff's residence, and the county jail. (From the collection of Joe Spear.)

Here is an early view of Chardon Savings Bank, located on Main Street near Water Street. Before metropolitan, regional, and national banks expanded to small-town America, Chardon's banking needs were served by locally owned financial institutions, with Chardon Savings Bank the largest and best known in the area. Today, Chardon is home to numerous branch offices of area banks. (From the collection of the Geauga County Archives.)

This building, the home of Chardon Savings Bank from the 1960s to the 1980s, was constructed on the site of the old Park Hotel. Later expanded, it now has three floors and contains the office of JP Morgan Chase and several other businesses. (From the collection of Bill Jackson.)

This is the storefront of Henry Bickle, an undertaker and furniture dealer. It was not uncommon for an individual to run these two businesses in parallel. Bickle's business was eventually sold and became one of the roots of today's Burr Funeral Home. (From the collection of Patricia Fisher Benedict.)

This is an early view of the house on South Street that became the Burr Funeral Home. Although significantly remodeled, features of the building seen in this photograph can still be identified in today's structure. The Burr Funeral Home is one of the oldest continuously operated family businesses in the area. (From the collection of Marc and Nan Burr.)

Here is an assortment of approximately 75 farm machines, including binders, mowers, and reapers, upon their delivery to Chardon in mid-May 1897. L.C. Cowles, local agent for the Champion Farm Implement Company, oversaw this delivery. (From the collection of the Geauga County Historical Society.)

This is a portrait of the Siska family on their farm in northeastern Chardon Township. The buildings in the background still exist and the farm is still owned by the family. This family was one of many first- and second-generation immigrant households that purchased and operated local farms after having lived and worked in Cleveland. (From the collection of Shirley Pokorny.)

The men of the Siska family use a steam-powered thresher to process grain on the family farm in northeastern Chardon Township. (From the collection of Shirley Pokorny.)

This photograph shows Corey Hospital, a private medical facility owned and operated by Dr. Walter C. Corey, which served Geauga County from about 1933 through the late 1950s. Primarily a children's hospital, as many as 250 deliveries were made here in a year. Located at 239 South Hambden Street in Chardon, Corey Hospital was later replaced by the county's first community hospital. (From the collection of Joe Spear.)

This image shows the John Williams grain and feed mill, located at the foot of Center Street, near the old railroad right-of-way. This mill was built in 1880 and served Chardon for several decades. The building was torn down in 1966. (From the collection of Joe Spear.)

This is a view of the Davis Block in the early 1900s. The block was completed in 1876. The complex housed Chardon's freight and passenger depot for the Cleveland & Eastern electric railroad. The arched doorway, shown here with milk cans in front of it, served as the freight station, with the passenger station to the right. (From the collection of the Geauga County Archives.)

Car No. 53 of the Cleveland & Eastern electric railroad sits in front of the freight and passenger depot at the south end of Chardon Square. This car was one of the "picture window" cars that provided unobstructed views of the Geauga County countryside on trips to and from Cleveland. The maple leaf insignia can be seen in the upper panes of the car's windows. (From the collection of Bill Jackson.)

A Cleveland & Eastern car approaches Chardon Square from South Street, with the Chardon House in the background. The name Chardon House dates this photograph as prior to 1912. This railroad made travel to Cleveland a far less arduous task and allowed local residents to conduct business or shop in the city and return on the same day. (From the collection of the Geauga County Archives.)

This is the trestle on the Cleveland & Eastern electric railroad as it passed over the tracks of the B&O railroad at the southwest corner of Chardon Village. The car on the trestle is headed east, toward South Street. A short spur located west of the trestle connected the electric railroad with the steam railroad and allowed the transfer of coal cars between the two lines. (From the collection of the Richards family.)

A Greyhound bus passes through Chardon in this image estimated to be from the 1940s. Following the dissolution of the electric railroad, a series of bus companies offered passenger service to the Chardon community. (From the collection of Fred Wilder.)

Some of the "telephone girls" employed by the Chardon Telephone Exchange pose for a photograph. The company started in 1895 and survived as an independent provider of telephone services for a number of decades before being purchased by the Western Reserve Telephone Company. (From the collection of Betty Talcott.)

The "telephone girls" work the switchboard of the Chardon Telephone Exchange as two male supervisors peer over the top of the equipment. (From the collection of Betty Talcott.)

The Chardon Telephone Company building was on South Hambden Street. The company later became part of the Western Reserve Telephone Company and was eventually sold to Windstream. (From the collection of the Geauga County Archives.)

The editor of the *Geauga Republican*, Dick Denton, and his assistant, Emma Cowle, are pictured here in the newspaper's Chardon office about 1915. This newspaper, along with its rival, the *Geauga Record*, was published in Chardon for many years. The two newspapers merged in 1921. (From the collection of Joe Spear.)

This group photograph shows the township reporters for the *Geauga Republican* about 1895. In order to receive current information from the townships of Geauga and Lake Counties, the local newspapers recruited correspondents from each township to provide weekly updates on the happenings in these locations. For a number of years, these reporters gathered for a summer outing. (From the collection of Joe Spear.)

A group of men pose in front of a Chardon barbershop and billiard parlor. (From the collection of Joe Spear.)

Chardon barbers work at their trade. The barbers are, from left to right, Lloyd Hendershott, Hal Greene, and Fred K. Hendershott. (From the collection of Joe Spear.)

The dry goods store of Clyde W. Goodrich was located on Main Street. Clyde Goodrich is pictured in the aisle on the left and Pearl Smith is behind the counter on the right. (From the collection of the Allyn family.)

The Eldredge jewelry store, pictured here, was also located on Main Street. (From the collection of Priscilla Eldredge.)

The interior of the Ben Franklin Store on Main Street is pictured here at a time when many small household items could be purchased for 5, 10, and 25 cents. (From the collection of Joe Spear.)

This is a very old photograph of the Canfield & Son grocery and the livery and harness business of J.O. Teed. (From the collection of Joe Spear.)

This is the delivery wagon of C.W. Whiston, Chardon butcher and meat dealer. (From the collection of Joe Spear.)

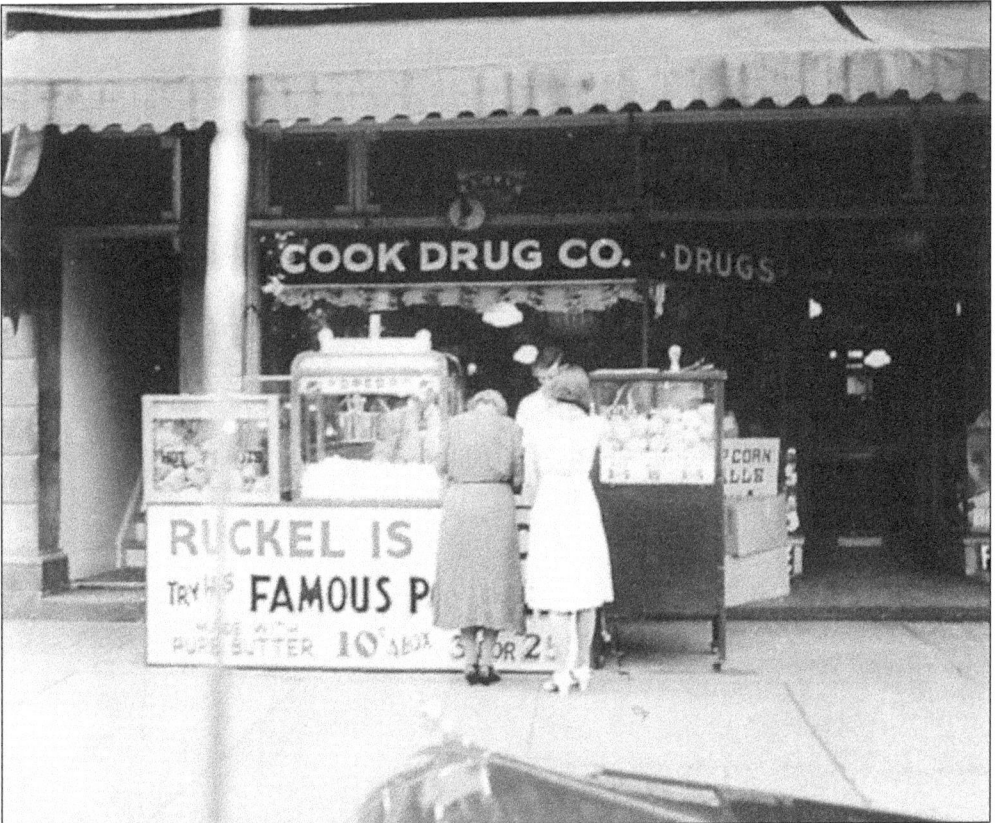

Ruckel's "seasonal" popcorn business was located on Main Street, in front of Cook Drug Co., when a public event was taking place in and around Chardon Square, such as the village's Saturday night concerts. (From the collection of the Rickard family.)

This is the counter at Rickard's Bakery, a favorite stop of many local residents for decades. (From the collection of Barbara and Milton Luther.)

In 2010, the Richards family celebrated its 100th year of selling maple products. In this photograph, one of the founders of the family business, Rena Welk Richards, sells bricks of maple sugar at an early Geauga County Maple Festival. (From the collection of the Richards family.)

Melvin Hossler is pictured here with his gasoline wagon. Hossler is known for his direct competition with the oil baron John D. Rockefeller. When Rockefeller tried to squeeze Hossler out of the oil distribution business, Hossler fought back and gained a loyal contingent of local patrons. (From the collection of the Geauga County Historical Society.)

This c. 1920 image shows the gasoline station of Melvin Hossler on Water Street, believed to be the first such station in the village. Hossler continued in the oil and gasoline business until his death in 1946. (From the collection of the Geauga County Historical Society.)

The hauling truck and trailer of S. Daniel and Son has a full load in front of the Chardon Post Office on Main Street. (From the collection of the Geauga County Historical Society.)

The hauling wagon of Melvin Hossler is loaded with household furnishings. Hossler, Chardon's well-known oil merchant, also transported local goods for a fee. (From the collection of Joe Spear.)

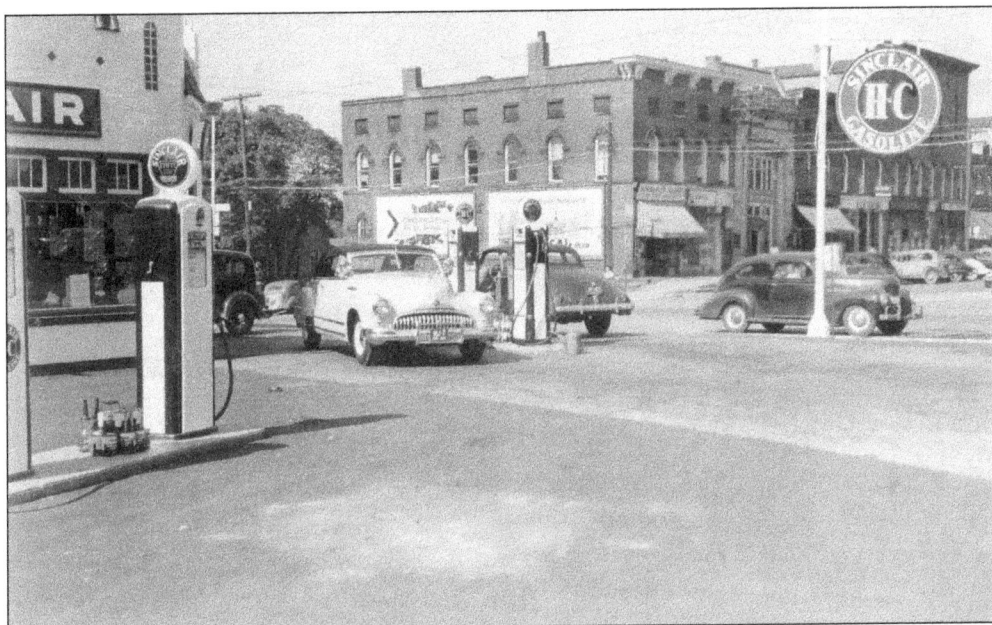

The Sinclair gasoline station was at the corner of South and Water Streets. Schinagle's meat market and Chardon Savings Bank are in the background. (From the collection of Jan Farinacci.)

Farinacci's Buick and Oldsmobile dealership was at the corner of South and Water Streets. (From the collection of Jan Farinacci.)

This is a view of Miller's Garage, at the north end of Chardon Square, with its tow truck. The garage was started by Harrison F. Miller, a former Chardon Disciple minister, around 1915. His son Kenneth later joined Harrison and took over the business until Kenneth's retirement in the 1970s. (From the collection of Joe Spear.)

In this early 1950s photograph, Chardon Village workers remove one of the last hitching posts on the northern section of Main Street. Wettstein's Bakery and Pastry Shop is in the background. (From the collection of Joe Spear.)

Five

Churches and Cemeteries

The residents of Chardon Village have long been supportive members of various Christian denominations and built places of worship in which to hold their services. In the early years, the primary denominations were Methodist, Baptist, Congregational, and Disciples of Christ. In the early 20th century, the Catholic church established a local presence. More recently, many other denominations have become part of the religious mix of the Chardon community.

Throughout the history of Chardon, almost all church buildings were located in the village. Even today, Chardon Township only has two churches.

The Chardon Baptist Church was constructed about 1840 and completed a few years later. This structure was located on East Park Street, south of the present-day Goodrich Court. The church building was abandoned about 1909, after its congregation dwindled in numbers. (From the collection of the Geauga County Historical Society.)

This is a later view of the Chardon Baptist Church after it ceased to function as a church, was sold to a private owner, and became an automobile dealership and repair garage. After leaving the furniture and undertaking business, Henry Bickle purchased the abandoned church building and converted it into a garage where he serviced the rapidly expanding population of automobile owners. (From the collection of Joe Spear.)

The first Chardon Methodist Church was a wood-framed structure built on the west side of Main Street, near where Memorial Hall was later located. The Chardon Methodist Church was organized in 1818. The building was started in 1833 and dedicated in 1836. As the first church building in Chardon, this church was awarded the bell provided by Peter Chardon Brooks. (From the collection of Joe Spear.)

The Chardon Methodist Church survived the great fire of 1868. As seen in this photograph, the church structure remained relatively unscathed, even though the Geauga County Courthouse to its left was a charred ruin. The last service was held in this building on December 20, 1883. (From the collection of Joe Spear.)

This brick structure on Main Street was the second of three buildings to house Chardon Methodist Church. A group of Sunday school students pose on the front steps of the church around 1910. (From the collection of Bill Jackson.)

This view of the second Chardon Methodist Church is from the early 1950s. The Western Auto store and the L.K. Burgess and Son grocery store are shown at left. (From the collection of Bill Jackson.)

The Disciple Church on South Street is seen here long before its merger with the First Congregational Church and before it was known as the Chardon Christian Church. The wood-frame building was constructed about 1861. The spire of the First Congregational Church is visible in the background. (From the collection of Bill Jackson.)

The new look of Chardon Christian Church is pictured here. Formerly known as the Disciple Church, the congregation altered its front by adding a concrete block face in 1911. Stained-glass windows were integrated into the project. Purchased by Chardon Village in 1991, this building was torn down in 1993. The stained-glass windows were sold at auction and acquired by local residents. (From the collection of Bill Jackson.)

This is a view of the First Congregational Church, with its tall spire, during the early 1900s. At various points in its history, this building has been with and without a steeple. The original steeple was removed before the Depression due to concerns over its structural stability. The most recent steeple was added in 1992. (From the collection of Bill Jackson.)

This photograph shows the First Congregational Church after 1930. The municipal water tower was in the background and this church building no longer had a spire on its west tower. (From the collection of Bill Jackson.)

The original location of St. Mary's Catholic Church was on the northwest corner of Cemetery Street and Ferris Avenue. The building was constructed in 1908, dedicated in 1910, and served the small Catholic community in Chardon at this location for almost 25 years. (From the collection of Joe Spear.)

The original St. Mary's building was relocated to North Street, next to the rectory. The structure was physically moved to this site in 1932; the move took place over Ferris Avenue, Water and Washington Streets, Fifth Avenue, and North Street. This church building, in slightly expanded form, was the parish's worship space until 1961, when a new church was built across the street. (From the collection of Bill Jackson.)

This is a c. 1910 view of the Chardon Municipal Cemetery. The mausoleum in the center of the photograph was built for the Eaton family. This cemetery has remained in continuous use, and burials still take place there. (From the collection of Bill Jackson.)

The dedication ceremony for the Chardon Municipal Cemetery Mausoleum took place in 1913 and had a moderate audience. Mayor H.C. Bickle presided over the dedication. It is not known if the umbrellas were for protection from the rain or from the sun. (From the collection of Joe Spear.)

Six

SCHOOLS

Public schools in Chardon Village and Chardon Township began operating in the mid-19th century. In 1873, the first consolidated school was built in Chardon Village to instruct students of all grade levels living in and around the village, including students of high school age. At the same time, Chardon Township was dotted with six small schoolhouses, each of which served a circle of families generally residing within a several-mile radius of the school. Older students attended Chardon High School. The tiny township schools remained in operation until the late 1930s, when the expanded Chardon school system began to operate consolidated elementary schools in Chardon as well as in neighboring Hambden and Munson Townships.

Chardon has a proud tradition of excellent schools and quality teachers. In addition, its citizens have generally supported their schools with the passage of levies and bond issues.

Maple Rock School was one of six one-room schoolhouses in Chardon Township during the late 1800s and early 1900s. This building is still located on Chardon Mentor Road, just south of Wisner Road. (From the collection of the Geauga County Archives.)

Pupils and their teacher are seen here during an early year at the Maple Rock School. (From the collection of the Geauga County Historical Society.)

The students and teacher at Protestant School are shown here during the 1935–1936 school year. This building was located at the southeast corner of Chardon-Painesville Road and Clark Road in the northern section of Chardon Township. (From the collection of Shirley Pokorny.)

Here is an early baseball game on the field at Protestant School in northern Chardon Township. The young man at bat is wearing his knickers. The schoolhouse and its outhouses are in the background, with the local cemetery behind them. (From the collection of Shirley Pokorny.)

This image shows the Chardon High School football team from 1920. The high school has been an active participant in the sports of football, basketball, baseball, and track and field since the early 1900s. In addition to a number of individual state champions, the school has fielded state championship teams in football and cross country. (From the collection of Karen Simpson.)

Chardon Center School was located just west of Auburn Road on Chardon Mentor Road. Center Street in Chardon was so named because it connected the village of Chardon to the small community of "Chardon Center," located at this intersection. (From the collection of Geauga County Public Library.)

This is an unobstructed photograph of the Union School, the building constructed in 1873 for the consolidation of Chardon schools. It was located on the site now occupied by Park Elementary School. The building housed the high school classes, as well as all lower grades. (From the collection of Joe Spear.)

The schoolyard of the Union School is seen here during a typical Chardon winter day in the 1897–1898 school year. Park Auditorium now occupies the schoolyard. The building on the right is the Chardon Town Hall. At times, the town hall was used to accommodate an oversized student population. It is clear that this photograph predates 1908, because there are no clock faces in the courthouse tower. (From the collection of Joe Spear.)

This is a photograph of the old Union School and the "new" building that was exclusively used for high school classes. The older building on the right was built to house all 12 grades. Authorized in 1872 and built in 1873, it was called the Union School because it brought all students, from first grade through 12th grade, into a single building. The superintendent during the early 1870s was W.S. Hayden. (From the collection of Bill Jackson.)

This pre-1900s photograph is of the older students and their teachers at the Union School. (From the collection of Joe Spear.)

Younger students pose in front of the Union School. The apparel may be of particular interest to those who enjoy vintage clothing. (From the collection of Joe Spear.)

In this c. 1911 image, the full student body of Chardon High School poses in front of the 1908 high school building. It is doubtful that students would be permitted to perch in the second-floor windows today. (From the collection of Bill Jackson.)

The 28-member Chardon High School Class of 1909 posed at the original gazebo on Chardon Square for a class photograph. This class was the first to graduate from the "new" high school building. (From the collection of Bill Jackson.)

A small class poses on the stage of the Opera House for graduation ceremonies. The class motto was "Sow, Then Reap." (From the collection of Joe Spear.)

The newly constructed Park Elementary and Park Auditorium are shown here about 1938. The auditorium was completed and put into use in late 1937. The high school is the building between the two new structures. (From the collection of Joe Spear.)

This view shows the second Chardon High School building in the early 1950s, shortly after its first phase of construction. The building had fewer classrooms in its early days than today's expanded structure. (From the collection of Bill Jackson.)

The first high school and Park Auditorium are shown here on a winter's day in the late 1930s. (From the collection of Fred Wilder.)

The Chardon High School orchestra is featured in this photograph taken in the late 1930s, within a year or two of its establishment. The picture was taken on the front lawn of Union School, prior to the building of Park Auditorium. (From the collection of Rob and Mazie Smith.)

Seven

PEOPLE AND
THEIR ACTIVITIES

The Chardon community has participated in a diverse spectrum of activities throughout the years, including many recreational, patriotic, and political pastimes and gatherings. The pleasant natural beauty of the area offers many outdoor opportunities. The Little Mountain resort community was a major summer destination for the wealthier members of society. Today, public parks and other recreational facilities provide easy access to fresh air activities.

The following photographs demonstrate not only the comfortable relationship of Chardon's citizens with Mother Nature, but also the community's strong sense of patriotism and its appreciation for music and other forms of entertainment.

A large group of Civil War veterans are pictured here on the steps of the Memorial Hall building. Over the course of the early 20th century, this group quickly dwindled in size as death called these aging men. This photograph was likely taken between 1910 and 1915. (From the collection of the Geauga County Archives.)

The top floor of Memorial Hall was dedicated to the veterans of the Civil War. The hall was used by the Grand Army of the Republic (a veterans' group) and the Woman's Relief Corps (its auxiliary). Erected in the summer of 1895, the structure was three stories high and measured 50 feet by 75 feet. (From the collection of Betty Meyer.)

The Chardon Cornet Band is shown here around 1882. The band performed during the last quarter of the 19th century. Etta Eldredge Sanger was the drummer. Chardon was well known for its musical talent, including Prof. Tillinghast Rogers, who composed many religious and patriotic works and instructed numerous young people in musical matters. (From the collection of Priscilla Eldredge.)

A uniformed Chardon Cornet Band played in front of the first gazebo around 1890. Chardon earned a reputation as a musical town and throughout its history has been supportive of local bands, orchestras, and singing groups. (From the collection of Joe Spear.)

This photograph shows a gathering of prospective military recruits on the steps of the Geauga County Courthouse around World War I. (From the collection of Joe Spear.)

From left to right, Columbus, Ohio, mayor James A. Rhodes; program chairman Wayne Johnson; and comedian Bob Hope are shown at the dedication of the Chardon Community Boosters' Club Memorial Field on October 8, 1948. The football field was constructed that summer to honor the local veterans of World Wars I and II. The field served the high school until the late 1990s, when it was replaced by the current Memorial Field. (From the collection of the Pentek family.)

In this photograph, a large crowd assembles at the south end of Chardon Square to send off a number of prospective military recruits during World War II. The bus was preparing to depart for Cleveland with a load of candidates. (From the collection of Rob and Mazie Smith.)

A patriotic crowd gathers inside the Opera House for an unknown event. This room occupied the second floor of the Smith Block and held up to 500 people. The Opera House opened in December 1875 with a Chardon Thespian Society performance of *The Sea of Ice*. Lucy Stone and James A. Garfield reportedly spoke here. Silent and talking motion pictures were shown here in the 1920s. (From the collection of the Geauga County Archives.)

This c. 1875 photograph shows a gathering of military veterans at the northern end of Chardon Square on Memorial Day. (From the collection of Joe Spear.)

Another Memorial Day remembrance is shown here around 1900. The Chardon chapter of the Odd Fellows and many schoolchildren make up a good portion of the marchers. (From the collection of Joe Spear.)

This is a Memorial Day procession from about 1920. The marchers turned from Main Street onto South Street as they made their way to the village cemetery. Today's marchers follow a similar route as they proceed from Park Auditorium, across Short Court Street, to Main and South Streets on their way to the cemetery. Several hundred participants take part each year. (From the collection of Priscilla Eldredge.)

This Memorial Day parade is at the south end of Main Street in the 1940s. The commemoration of Memorial Day with a ceremony and parade continues in Chardon today. (From the collection of Bill Jackson.)

This photograph shows the Geauga County Centennial Celebration parade in 1905. Chardon, as the county seat of Geauga County, hosted this event that attracted attendees from throughout the county. Note the Cleveland & Eastern electric railroad tracks at right, on the perimeter of the southern half of Chardon Square. Many of the revelers would have arrived on its interurban cars. (From the collection of Joe Spear.)

This pleasant image shows the activities in the Village Park during the 1905 Geauga County Centennial Celebration. The 1875 gazebo was patriotically decorated, an interurban car rested on Main Street, attendees wandered through the park, and vendors sold from concession stands in the background. (From the collection of Joe Spear.)

Here the members of the Congregational Church of Chardon stage a production of *Belle of Baghdad*. Over the years, the churches of Chardon have provided many musical and theatrical entertainments for their congregations and the community, most often performed by local talent. (From the collection of the Chardon Chamber of Commerce.)

Little Mountain Club members could visit this lookout on a clear day for a view west to Cleveland and north to Lake Erie. (From the collection of the Lake County Historical Society.)

This sketch depicts the Little Mountain Eagle, a short-lived hotel on top of Little Mountain. No known photograph exists. After just a few years, the owner abandoned the business, allowing the structure to degrade. It was eventually torn down. (From the collection of the Lake County Historical Society.)

A group of well-dressed guests pose in front of the Pine Crest Hotel. The guests were standing in Lake County, with the hotel straddling the Lake and Geauga County line. The structure, built in 1892, was the last Little Mountain hotel to serve the public, but it only survived as a going concern for about 20 years. (From the collection of the Lake County Historical Society.)

This is a full view of the Pine Crest Hotel from the northwest. This large structure had a rustic charm, but fell out of favor as the wealthy and the well-to-do began to go farther afield for their vacations. By the early 1900s, it was all but abandoned by summer visitors. (From the collection of the Lake County Historical Society.)

Paul Denton (on the piano) and his orchestra played at many events in Chardon from the 1940s until the 1960s. At wedding receptions, fraternal gatherings, and public celebrations, vocal and instrumental music has been a constant element in Chardon's social life. (From the collection of the Chardon Chamber of Commerce.)

This is an early photograph of the Stebbins family cabin at Stebbins Gulch, a beautiful creek valley in western Chardon Township. The gulch is now owned by the Holden Arboretum and is listed in the National Register of Historic Places. The Holden Arboretum periodically schedules public walks into Stebbins Gulch to explore this unique natural setting. (From the collection of Bill Jackson.)

This bandstand was located on the southern half of Chardon Square in the early 1950s. The original, more ornate gazebo, built about 1875, was torn down in the late 1930s due to disrepair. The gazebo was replaced by this simple octagonal platform with railings. The dedication took place on June 24, 1939. A third bandstand, designed to closely replicate the original, was dedicated on November 8, 1981. (From the collection of Bill Jackson.)

This is an early photograph of a Chardon Boy Scout troop. The Boy Scouts organization was started in America in 1910; this picture was likely taken very soon thereafter. (From the collection of the Geauga County Archives.)

A Conestoga wagon passes through Chardon during the sesquicentennial celebration of the establishment of the Northwest Territory. The Northwest Ordinance was enacted in 1787 and a territorial government was formed in Marietta on July 15, 1788. A major event in the 150th-year commemoration was this wagon caravan from Massachusetts to Marietta, Ohio, that concluded on April 7, 1938. (From the collection of Fred Wilder.)

Massachusetts senator Jack Kennedy and his wife, Jackie, sample Geauga County maple syrup at the Main Street offices and home of the county sheriff Louis Robusky in April 1959. Robusky was one of the few county Democratic office holders at this time. Kennedy was considering seeking the Democratic nomination for president. (From the collection of John Reithoffer.)

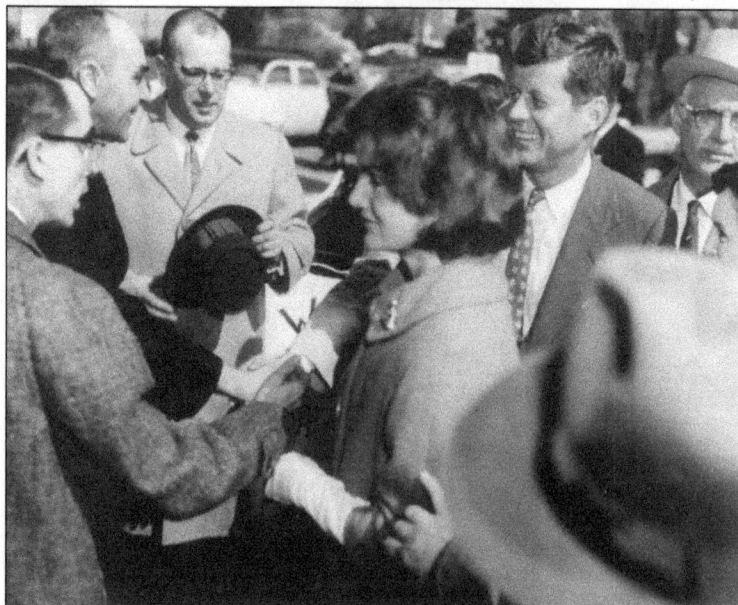

In this image, the Kennedys shake hands with Geauga County dignitaries, including Bob Smith (extending hand) and local Democratic Party chairman John Reithoffer (holding hat). (From the collection of Rob and Mazie Smith.)

Eight

MAPLE SUGAR INDUSTRY

At one time, Geauga County was the largest producer of maple sugar and syrup products in the nation. During the first quarter of the 20th century, the county shipped its products to places such as Vermont and other New England states to help satisfy the demand in those locations. In the process of shipping, it is understood that the Geauga County origin of the products was sometimes unidentified. In 1926, local merchant A.B. Carlson, concerned that the producers of Geauga County were not receiving adequate credit for their labors, conceived the idea of a local festival to celebrate maple syrup production within Geauga County. Thus, a tradition was born that continues into its ninth decade.

While Ohio and Geauga County have gradually become lesser players in the maple syrup market, the agricultural product still provides a major activity and income for a number of farmers in the late winter and early spring. As part of growing up in Geauga County, many young folks experiment with tapping maple trees and boiling the maple sap they collect to produce syrup and candies.

This young man distributes sap buckets around a sugar bush on the Canyon Valley Farm at Little Mountain in 1914. A sugar bush is a local expression for a grove of sugar maple trees. (From the collection of the Lake County Historical Society.)

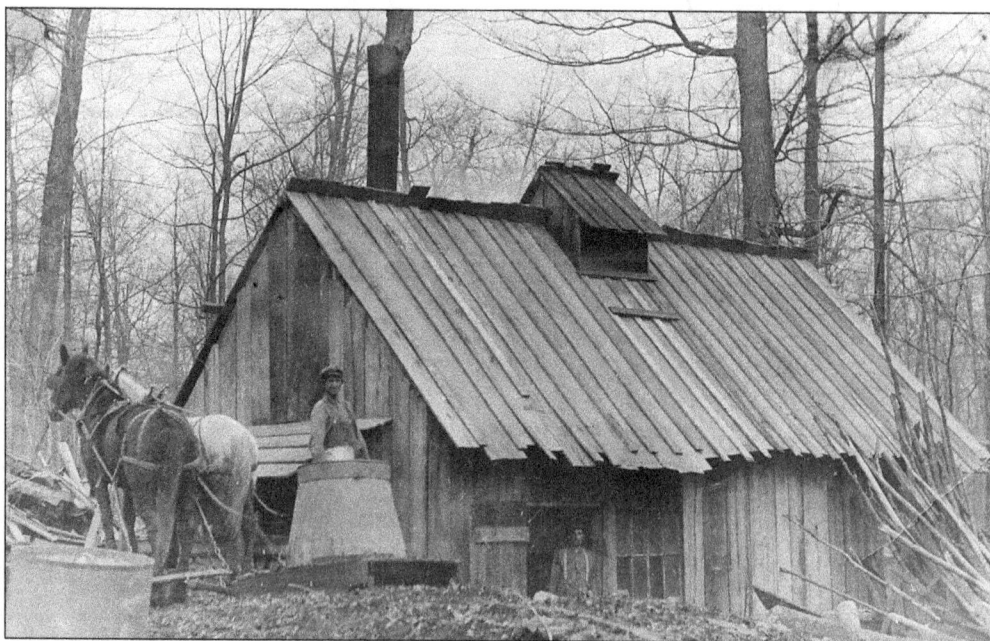

This man, his horse team, and sled had just collected the day's run of sap and were in the process of delivering it to a sugarhouse in Chardon Township. The sap was then boiled to reduce the water content. It takes 40 to 50 gallons of sap to make a single gallon of maple syrup. (From the collection of Bill Jackson.)

The sugaring season can be quite unpredictable. Freezing overnight temperatures need to contrast with warmer daytime temperatures to provide a steady flow of sap. A cold winter can delay the start of the maple syrup season, while snow and rain can make servicing the sugar bush difficult. Unusually warm temperatures can greatly shorten the period of sap collection. Here a young man pours a bucket of sap into the collection container. No snow is on the ground. (From the collection of Shirley Pokorny.)

The old sugarhouse on the Chardon Lakes Golf Course, off Woodiebrook Road, is shown here. Like other sugar camps, the sugarhouse collected sap from the surrounding sugar maple trees and boiled it down into a variety of maple syrup and maple sugar products. (From the collection of Bill Jackson.)

This early postcard depicts costumed "pioneers" making maple syrup the old-fashioned way, in an outdoor evaporator fueled by large quantities of seasoned wood. (From the collection of Bill Jackson.)

Maple syrup has been made by generations of Geauga County residents. Here, two young boys boil sap in a primitive lean-to of their own making. Many Chardon youth experiment with making syrup. (From the collection of Betty Koelliker.)

At an early Geauga County Maple Festival, workers gather sap on Chardon Square using a sled pulled by oxen. The homes that formerly lined East Park Street are visible in the background. (From the collection of Jerry Tvergyak.)

A young man watches over a long evaporator used in boiling sap. (From the collection of the Geauga County Archives.)

Lynn Hosford tends the demonstration evaporator in the sugarhouse on Chardon Square during the Geauga County Maple Festival. (From the collection of Joe Spear.)

During the early years of the Geauga County Maple Festival, a large exhibition building was erected on Short Court Street. This building housed displays and merchandise associated with the event. The 180-foot-long building was assembled and disassembled for a number of festivals and was last used about 1931. (From the collection of Fred Wilder.)

This photograph shows the exhibition hall during an early Geauga County Maple Festival, offering a rare glimpse at the event without the presence of snow or rain. (From the collection of Fred Wilder.)

The Rube Band performs during a 1940s Geauga County Maple Festival. (From the collection of Fred Wilder.)

Here, the ox team and cart of Harry and Lana Stanton circles Chardon Square during a 1950s Geauga County Maple Festival parade. (From the collection of Bill Jackson.)

A log-cutting contest, using axes, was held during an early 1950s Geauga County Maple Festival. The row of houses that once lined East Park Street, including the Smith house, one-time home of the *Geauga Times Leader*, is behind the crowd of onlookers. (From the collection of Priscilla Eldredge.)

Gladys Strong McDonald, the queen of the first Geauga County Maple Festival, held in 1926, is pictured here with the 1960 festival queen, Margaret Daniels (right). The Maple Festival Queens are selected from a pool of local applicants. (From the collection of Dottie Wedge.)

The Geauga County Maple Festival hosts an annual dinner for the senior citizens of the community. In this photograph from the early 1950s, the honorees posed within the Pilgrim Christian Church. Ohio governor Frank Lausche is seated at far right in the front row. (From the collection of Betty Koelliker.)

Here is an aerial view of the festival, showing the layout of the amusements and rides set up on Chardon Square. (From the collection of Joe Spear.)

A carousel ride from an early festival is seen here. Amusement rides have long been a tradition at the Geauga County Maple Festival. Those individuals willing to brave the cold weather purchase discounted tickets on Thursdays, the opening day of the festival, and ride throughout the evening. (From the collection of Mary Alice Taylor.)

Nine

SNOW CAPITAL

Chardon is known far and wide for the significant snowfall it receives each winter. Records covering the past 59 winters indicate that the average snowfall has been almost 108 inches per year. However, accumulations of 140 inches or more occur every few years. The most recent example of a snowy winter occurred during the winter of 2010–2011, when Chardon got 151 inches of snow. Perhaps the biggest recorded snow event was the snowstorm of November 1913, which blanketed Chardon with over four feet of snow in a three-day period. Travel was virtually impossible and commerce came to a standstill for several days. Another example was the pre-Thanksgiving storm in 1996 that dropped 63 inches of snow in two days.

The heavy snows occur because of the confluence of three major factors. Chardon lies about 11 miles south of Lake Erie, and as long as the lake remains unfrozen, the air that passes over it is exposed to its moisture. In the winter, winds from the west and northwest drive the moisture-laden clouds over Chardon. Finally, Chardon is located over 700 feet above the level of the lake. As the moist clouds pass over the higher elevation, their contents are often released, falling on the rolling hills of northern Geauga County. This "lake effect" snow condition occurs in very few locations in the world.

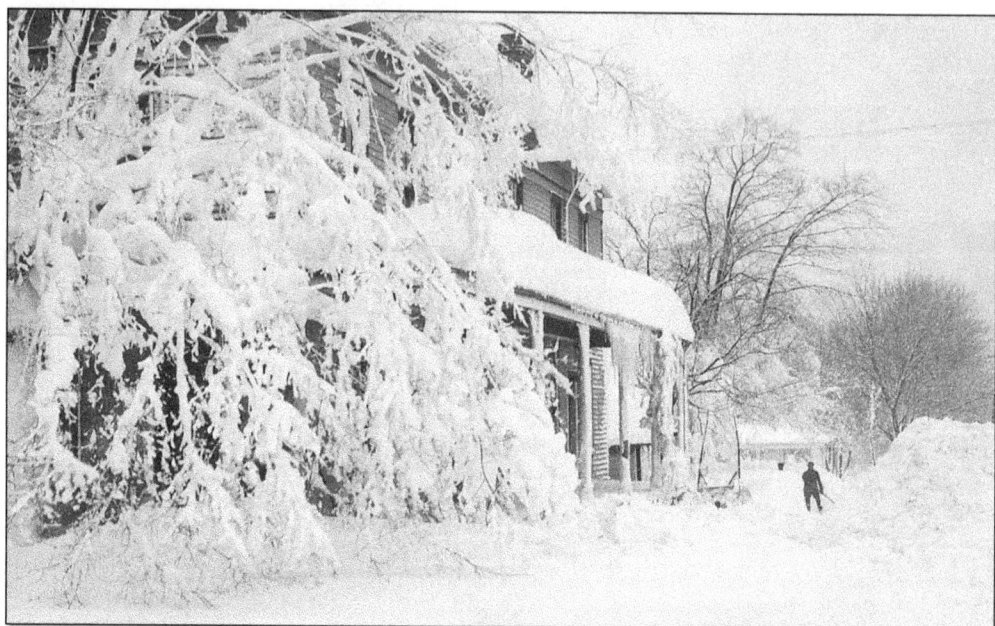

There were no motorized sidewalk plows or snowblowers in the early 1900s. The year 1913 was a very strange weather year. In April, Ohio and other states experienced some of the worst flooding in history, with a large loss of life. On November 9–12, much of northern Ohio was blanketed with a snowfall that paralyzed travel and commercial activity for up to a week. This photograph records the snow deposited by that November storm. (From the collection of Bill Jackson.)

This view of the results of the November 1913 snowstorm shows the snowplow of the day—two horses, two men, and a hand plow. The storm took place during the heyday of the postcard, and these snow scenes were captured by local photographer Stuart D. Strong and made into postcards that were then widely distributed and collected. (From the collection of Bill Jackson.)

This photograph of the south end of Main Street shows the aftermath of the November 1913 blizzard. It was reported that 32 inches of snow fell on Sunday night (November 9, 1913), and another 18 inches fell on Monday, November 10, 1913. The young work crew cut a meandering path through the snowfall to provide access to stores and businesses. The Highland Hotel is in the background. (From the collection of Bill Jackson.)

Eight- and nine-foot mounds of snow stood along Main Street in the aftermath of the November 1913 snowstorm. The mounds were the result of backbreaking labor by individuals with shovels. The H.F. Goodrich grocery store is shown in the background. (From the collection of Bill Jackson.)

Fleet Smith (on skis) and Hal Burr survey the results of the November 1913 snowstorm. (From the collection of Marc and Nan Burr.)

This is a view of the cleared sidewalk in front of the sheriff's office and retail establishments following the November 1913 snowstorm. The ladder propped against the building indicates that snow-shoveling likely took place on the rooftop as well. (From the collection of Bill Jackson.)

With the sidewalks cleared following the November 1913 blizzard, the townspeople escaped their homes and resumed patronizing the shops and businesses on Main Street. Other than walking, the only available modes of transportation in the days immediately following a snowstorm this severe were horses and sleighs or bobsleds. (From the collection of Bill Jackson.)

The sidewalk path shown here was merely a narrow passageway in a tunnel of snow. Before motorized plows, civic-minded men and boys would gather to perform the strenuous task of clearing the snow by hand and with simple machines. Similarly, teams of workers were engaged to remove snow from the tracks of the electric railroad after heavy snowfalls. (From the collection of Joe Spear.)

This is a long view of Main Street after the snowstorm of November 1913. Although the mounds of snow indicate that the sidewalk had been cleared, there was only a narrow path cut in the street and no indication of large-scale vehicle travel. (From the collection of Bill Jackson.)

A hardy snow-shoveler at the John Warner house on South Hambden Street carves a path through the snow deposited by the November 1913 snowstorm. Today, homeowners are responsible for clearing the sidewalks in front of their homes, although substantial assistance is provided by the city's motorized sidewalk snowplow. (From the collection of Joe Spear.)

This early 1913 image is another example of the wintertime presence of snow in Chardon. Today, modern machines plow the city's sidewalks. The meandering path shown in this photograph was created with hand shovels and the labor of citizens of the community. (From the collection of Joe Spear.)

This snowy view was photographed from the corner of the Highland Hotel at Water and South Streets looking south in November 1913. The Chardon Christian Church is on the left. Depending on the "wetness" of the snow, severe damage to trees may result. Here the trees are heavily coated with snow and their branches are bending near the breaking point. (From the collection of Karen Simpson.)

In this 1940s photograph, a tractor was used to clear the snow from the entrance to City Hall, which contained the offices of the Chardon police and fire departments. The First Congregational Church is on the left. At the time, the Village Restaurant was owned and operated by the Wettstein family. (From the collection of Joe Spear.)

Short Court Street is shown here with a moderate dusting of snow. While snow does not always remain on the ground in Chardon throughout the winter season, it is not unusual to have a measurable snow cover for significant portions of December, January, and February. (From the collection of Fred Wilder.)

Heavy snows in Chardon are not a rare occurrence. When this photograph was taken, just one lane of the roadway had been carved out for automobile travel—no doubt resulting in some interesting negotiations between travelers heading in opposite directions. The Chardon and Chardon Township community is proud of its service forces, which arduously work to keep the roads open. (From the collection of the Geauga County Archives.)

A snow-blowing plow truck at the south end of Chardon Square makes its rounds following a "snow event" in the late 1940s. At this time, the A&P grocery store was located on Main Street, along with the Eldredge Popcorn Co. and the Schinagle Market. (From the collection of Joe Spear.)

Members of the Chardon Ski Club in the early 1900s included, from left to right, Hal Burr, Harold Bostwick, Audrey Cook, Kenneth Miller, Warner Cook, and Stuart Austin. (From the collection of Joe Spear.)

This image shows the lighted bandstand on Chardon Square on a typical Chardon winter night. (From the collection of Joe Spear.)

Ten

CHARDON CENTENNIAL

The Chardon Centennial Celebration was held over three days—Thursday, July 25; Friday, July 26; and Saturday, July 27, 1912—to commemorate the founding of Chardon Township and the settlement of Chardon 100 years earlier. An energetic program of entertainments, activities, parades, and prizes filled the entire three days, drawing crowds not only from Chardon and Chardon Township, but from elsewhere in Geauga County and beyond.

The citizens of the day provided a wonderful commemoration of the founding of Chardon and left a splendid photographic history of the event, as evidenced by the following examples.

The arch at the Chardon Centennial Celebration is seen here on a quiet morning before the start of the day's festivities. After celebrating Geauga County's 100th anniversary just seven years earlier, the citizens of Chardon were determined to carry out a three-day commemoration of their own. (From the collection of Bill Jackson.)

This is a view of the Centennial Arch during the merchants parade on Thursday, July 25, 1912. The truck in the foreground is the entry of merchant H.F. Goodrich. (From the collection of Joe Spear.)

The marshal of the Chardon Centennial Celebration parade, Dr. S.G. Downing, sits on his horse at Chardon Square during the weekend's festivities. Doctor Downing was a dentist. Two aides, Bert Presley and Charles Ross, assisted the marshal in his official role. (From the collection of Joe Spear.)

The wagon of L.L. Fletcher, dry goods dealer, appeared in the Chardon Centennial Celebration merchants parade carrying a load of sheep and advertising Clothcraft All-Wool Clothes. While the exact location of the photograph is not known, based on the railroad cars in the background, it seems to have been taken near the lower section of Cemetery Street (now Park Avenue). (From the collection of Bill Jackson.)

The parade wagon of N.S. Battles advertised his "Dressed Beef" business. Here, the wagon is seen on Tilden Avenue in advance of the merchants parade. The Battles float was one of about 30 floats associated with Chardon businesses that participated in the parade. (From the collection of Joe Spear.)

This is the promotional parade wagon of local grocer L.M. Latimer. The float advertised Chase & Sanborn coffee and tea products. The participants in the merchants parade formed their procession on Tilden Avenue and Cemetery Street. (From the collection of Joe Spear.)

This is the decorated cart of Clara Fleet, who owned a millinery shop in Chardon for many years, preparing to take part in the merchants parade. (From the collection of the Geauga County Archives.)

The wagon of Burr and Smith, undertakers and furniture dealers, prepares to take part in the merchants parade on Thursday, July 25, 1912. (From the collection of Joe Spear.)

A florally decorated automobile shaped like a cake participated in the Chardon Centennial Celebration automobile parade. Automobile owner Clyde Goodrich (at the wheel) and his family are shown riding in the "cake." The vehicle rested on South Street, just south of Chardon Square. (From the collection of Bill Jackson.)

This float, advertising the strength of the Ford automobile, was loaded with as many as 30 young boys during the Chardon Centennial Celebration. Here, the car sits at the South Street end of Cemetery Street (now Park Avenue). The home of Dr. Ralph Pease is visible in the background. (From the collection of Joe Spear.)

122

A highly decorated car driven by its owner, E.A. Cook, and holding 10 children rests under the Centennial Arch on Main Street at the Chardon Centennial Celebration. This car, with a large butterfly on the front and two doves above the windshield, won second prize in the automobile parade on Saturday, July 27, 1912. (From the collection of Bill Jackson.)

A motorized canoe containing three costumed Indians—the family of Dr. Ralph Pease—heads north on South Street during the Chardon Centennial Celebration parade. The two houses in the background were located immediately north of Moffet Avenue. The Cleveland & Eastern electric railroad tracks are visible on the east side of the street, behind the canoe. (From the collection of Bill Jackson.)

The float called The Whitney, with its crew of six young ladies and a male driver, participates in the Chardon Centennial Celebration automobile parade. (From the collection of Bill Jackson.)

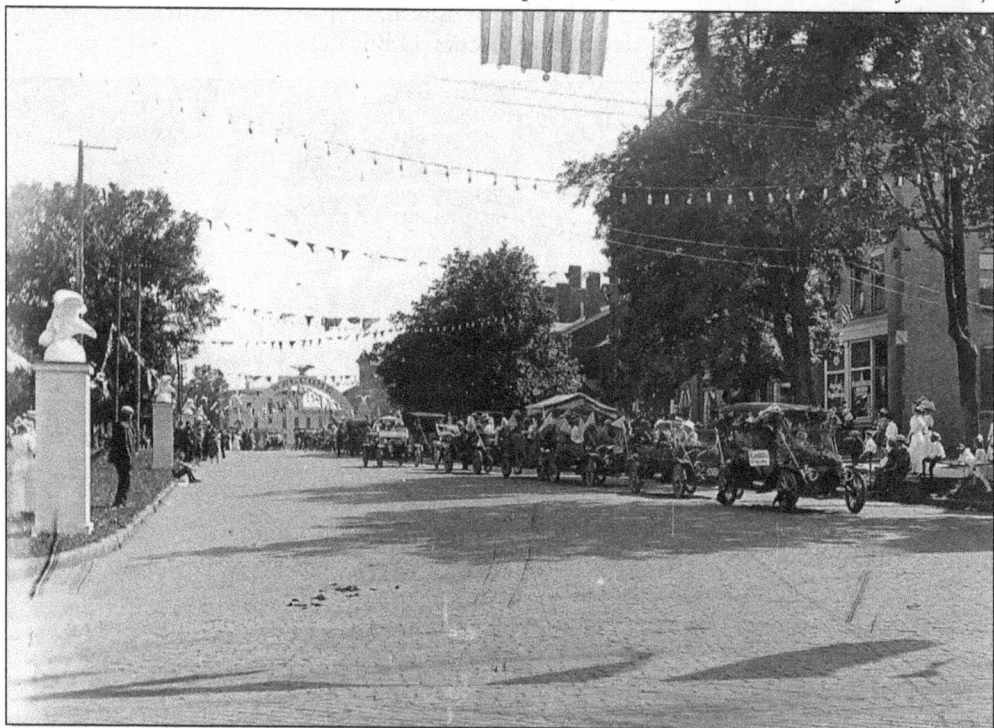

A squadron of decorated automobiles passes from Main Street onto Center Street during the Chardon Centennial Celebration. The automobile parade took place on Saturday, July 27, 1912. The building behind the lead car on the right housed the village's two newspapers, the *Geauga Republican* and the *Geauga Record*. (From the collection of Joe Spear.)

A highly decorated automobile owned by H.C. Parsons and populated with four young costumed fairies parks under the Centennial Arch at the Chardon Centennial Celebration. This car's decorations took first place in the automobile parade, held on Saturday, July 27, 1912. (From the collection of Bill Jackson.)

A giant swan float, guided by an underage driver, is shown on South Street at the start of the Saturday automobile parade during the Chardon Centennial Celebration. (From the collection of Joe Spear.)

Cattle and oxen pull a pair of carts at the Chardon Centennial Celebration. Henry Stone (left) led the first team, followed by Bill Walters and his oxen. An advertisement for a future "Grange Park" event is visible in the background. (From the collection of Joe Spear.)

A hot air balloon, piloted by Cleveland's Luna Park balloonist Charles E. Bankston, ascends on Chardon Square during the Chardon Centennial Celebration. Bankston performed a couple of ascensions over the course of the celebration. (From the collection of Joe Spear.)

Lionel Legare performed his famous spiral-tower balancing act on several occasions during the Chardon Centennial Celebration at Chardon Square. Here, a large crowd gathers in the park to watch his show. (From the collection of Bill Jackson.)

The Centennial Arch is illuminated by incandescent light bulbs at night. The electricity was provided by Chardon's own power plant. (From the collection of Joe Spear.)

Visit us at
arcadiapublishing.com

www.ingramcontent.com/pod-product-compliance
Lightning Source LLC
Chambersburg PA
CBHW080609110426
42813CB00006B/1450